A FIREFLY BOOK

Published by Firefly Books Ltd. 2014

First printing

Publisher Cataloging-in-Publication Data (U.S.)
Earley, Chris.
    Weird frogs / Chris Earley.
[64] p. : col. photos. ; cm.
Includes index.
Summary: Explores the weird and wonderful world of frogs through images and descriptions of their behavior and features.
ISBN-13: 978-1-77085-442-0
ISBN-13: 978-1-77085-361-4 (pbk.)
1. Frogs – Juvenile literature. 2. Frogs – Behavior – Juvenile literature. I. Title.
597.89 dc23   QL668.E2E365   2014

Library and Archives Canada Cataloguing in Publication
Earley, Chris G., 1968-, author
    Weird frogs / Chris Earley.
Includes index.
ISBN 978-1-77085-442-0 (bound).--ISBN 978-1-77085-361-4 (pbk.)
1. Frogs--Juvenile literature. 2. Frogs--Behavior--Juvenile literature. I. Title.
QL668.E2E37 2014   j597.8'9   C2014-901159-8

Published in the United States by
Firefly Books (U.S.) Inc.
P.O. Box 1338, Ellicott Station
Buffalo, New York 14205

Published in Canada by
Firefly Books Ltd.
50 Staples Avenue, Unit 1
Richmond Hill, Ontario L4B 0A7

IMAGE CREDITS
Front cover © Eric Isselee / Shutterstock; page 4 © Fablok / Shutterstock; page 5 © Hintau Aliaksei / Shutterstock; page 6 © MYN / Joris van Alphen / naturepl.com; page 7 © Eric Isselee / Shutterstock; page 8 © Aleksey Stemmer / Shutterstock; page 9 © tea maeklong / Shutterstock; page 10 © Eric Isselee / Shutterstock; page 11 © Panachai Cherdchucheep / Shutterstock; page 12–13 © Chris Mattison / naturepl.com; page 14 © Dr. Morley Read / Shutterstock; page 15 © Eric Isselee / Shutterstock; page 16 © Dirk Ercken / Shutterstock; page 17 © fivespots / Shutterstock; page 18 © Sandesh Kadur / naturepl.com; page 19 © MYN / Seth Patterson / naturepl.com; page 20 © fivespots / Shutterstock; page 21 © Cathy Keifer / Shutterstock; page 22 © J.Blanco / Shutterstock; page 23 © Morales / maXximages.com; page 24 © raulbaenacasado / Shutterstock; page 25 © Visuals Unlimited / naturepl.com; page 26 © Visuals Unlimited / naturepl.com; page 27 © Jorgen Larsson / imageselect; page 28–29 © Boaz Meiri / National Geographic; page 30 © Michael & Patricia Fogden / Minden Pictures; page 31 © Bert Willaert / naturepl.com; page 32 © IrinaK / Shutterstock; page 33 © Kim Taylor / Shutterstock; page 34 © Pan Xunbin / Shutterstock; page 35 © Visuals Unlimited / naturepl.com; page 36 © Dr. Morley Read / Shutterstock; page 37 © Visuals Unlimited / naturepl.com; page 38 © Aleksey Stemmer / Shutterstock; page 39 © fivespots / Shutterstock; page 40 © MYN / Joris van Alphen / naturepl.com; page 41 © Stanley Breeden / DRK; page 42 © Bert Willaert / naturepl.com; page 43 © Dr. Morley Read / Shutterstock; page 44 © Pete Oxford / Minden Pictures; page 45 © Eric Isselee / Shutterstock; page 46 © ARCO / naturepl.com; page 47 © Visuals Unlimited / naturepl.com; page 48 © Kim Taylor / naturepl.com; page 49 © Ryan M. Bolton / Shutterstock; page 50 © Matteo photos / Shutterstock; page 51 © Stephen Dalton / naturepl.com; page 52 © Dirk Ercken / Shutterstock; page 53 © Arto Hakola / Shutterstock; page 54 © reptiles4all / Shutterstock; page 55 © reptiles4all / Shutterstock; page 56 © Vitalii Hulai / Shutterstock; page 57 © Pete Oxford / naturepl.com; page 58 © MYN / Brady Beck / naturepl.com; page 59 © Chris Mattison / naturepl.com; page 60 © Nick Garbutt / naturepl.com; page 61 © Ryan M. Bolton / Shutterstock; page 62 © Claudio Contreras / naturepl.com; page 63 © Chris Mattison / naturepl.com; Back cover, right © Eric Isselee / Shutterstock; Back cover, left © Pete Oxford / Minden Pictures.

The publisher gratefully acknowledges the financial support for our publishing program by the Government of Canada through the Canada Book Fund as administered by the Department of Canadian Heritage.

Cover and interior design by Jacqueline Hope Raynor

Printed in China

INTRODUCTION

As a child I loved frogs. I caught them and watched them all the time. I marveled at the variation between different species: the dryness of a toad, the hugeness of a bullfrog, the toe pads on a tree frog. I can remember as a six year old seeing a toad, quick as a flash, catch and eat a tent caterpillar. I can also remember going to a fancy restaurant as an eight year old and seeing frogs' legs on the menu. Thinking it was a fun name like "buffalo wings," I ordered them. When they came to the table and I saw that they were real frogs' legs, I was horrified! I refused to eat them, telling my family that frogs were my friends.

Frogs now need as many friends as they can get. In recent decades, many frog populations have declined dramatically or disappeared altogether. Factors such as habitat loss, collecting for the pet trade, pollution, climate change and the introduction of invasive species are all contributing to the decimation of many frog species. A fungus called *Batrachochytrium dendrobatidis* has also spread around the world and caused the extinctions of some kinds of frogs. Research is underway to save the remaining species of frogs that are under threat but much remains to be done.

There are almost 6,000 species of frogs and toads and more are being discovered every year. They share the amphibian group with caecilians (which are legless and wormlike) and salamanders. The terms "frog" and "toad" are not taxonomic divisions: this means, for example, that not all toads are closely related. The word "toad" is often given to the ones that are dry-skinned and more terrestrial, whereas "frog" is for the slimy and more aquatic members of the group. But even this rough definition has many exceptions and so most are called frogs when talking about the group as a whole.

The more you know about the natural world around you, the better you will understand its intricacies and how our actions affect everything else that shares this world with us. And what better way to get started learning about the natural world than studying these frogs? They are so weird! Here is a group of animals that include jumpers, climbers, burrowers and even gliders. Some are poisonous, some are masters of camouflage and most are incredible vocalists. Their wide grins and large eyes attract our attention and they are one of the most recognizable animal groups on the planet. As you can see, I never really outgrew my frog stage. I hope this book encourages a life long frog stage for you, too.

MARSH FROG

Pelophylax ridibundus

This average-looking frog shows us that, really, every frog and toad is pretty weird. For one thing, there are very few true jumping animals. And most of those, such as kangaroos, rabbits and grasshoppers, are vegetarians. Frogs are jumping predators. Also, that massive mouth for swallowing their prey whole and those bulging eyes for seeing prey and predators are pretty strange, too.

EUROPEAN GREEN TOAD

Bufo viridis

Frogs and toads are amphibians called anurans, which means "without a tail." In general, the word "frog" tends to be used for anurans that are moist and smooth and the word "toad" for anurans that are dry and warty. The European Green Toad is a very pretty toad that can often be found under porch lights or street lights at night. The lights attract moths and other insects that the toad likes to eat.

ASIAN HORNED FROG

Megaphrys nasuta

While you may initially think those pointy eyebrows are there to make this frog look more fearsome to predators, they are actually doing just the opposite. The sharp points and ridges on the face and back make this Asian Horned Frog look like a fallen leaf so it can hide from predators.

ORIENTAL FIRE-BELLIED TOAD

Bombina orientalis
Like the unrelated Poison Dart Frogs, Fire-bellied Toads have toxins in their skin and they warn potential predators of this with their bright colors. To make sure that a predator really knows that they are poisonous, the toads may even arch their backs to show off their fiery red bellies.

AFRICAN BULLFROG

Pyxicephalus adspersus
This frog spends much of its time in burrows waiting for rain. When water does collect in puddles or low spots, the frog comes out of its burrow to breed. The female lays three to four thousand eggs and the male often stays to defend the eggs and tadpoles by puffing itself up and jumping at predators to scare them away!

ASIAN BULLFROG

Kaloula pulchra
This tropical bullfrog is very adaptable and has become a common sight during the rainy season in small towns in Southern Asia. It is also called the Chubby Frog because of its round body shape. If it feels threatened, it can puff itself up to look more formidable to a predator.

GIANT MONKEY FROG

Phyllomedusa bicolor
This large tree frog has flash markings on the undersides of its legs and sides. These orange and white markings, it is thought, help the frog survive since a predator chasing the frog will focus on these markings when the frog jumps. But, when the frog lands, it pulls its legs in which covers the markings and it now looks like a leaf, leaving the predator looking for a pattern that has disappeared.

TREE FROG

Family Hylidae
Many tree frogs have very weird toes. The round disc at the tip of each toe is covered with a microscopic honeycomb of columns that allow the frogs to hold on to rough surfaces such as bark. On smooth surfaces, the toes use mucus to create surface tension to help them hold on.

PAINTED-BELLY LEAF FROG

Phyllomedusa sauvagii
Most tree frogs live in wet rain forest habitats. But
the Painted-belly Leaf Frog is found in a hot, dry area
of South America. It stops itself from drying out by
covering its skin with a waxy substance from special
skin glands. This coating allows it to live in conditions
that would cause other frogs to dry up and die.

STRAWBERRY POISON DART FROG

Dendrobates pumilio
This species of Poison Dart Frog can be quite variable in appearance.
Color combinations include base colors of red, blue, green or yellow
in combination with different colored legs or body spots. But the
message is still the same: the colors tell predators to leave the
poisonous frogs alone or they will regret it!

GOLDEN POISON DART FROG

Phyllobates terribilis

This frog may be the most poisonous animal on the planet. One individual frog can contain enough poison to kill 20,000 mice or seven humans! South American Indians wipe the points of their darts on the frog's back, making the darts very deadly. They blow the darts through a long, hollowed out piece of wood to launch them at the animals they hunt. As their name suggests, Golden Poison Dart Frogs are often bright yellow but some populations have a minty green color.

TWIN-SPOTTED GLIDING FROG

Rhacophorus bipunctatus
This gliding frog shows extensive webbing on the
front feet. This webbing, along with that on the back
feet, helps the frog stay aloft as they jump from one
tree to another. Twin-spotted Gliding Frogs are one
of the smaller species of gliding frogs.

MEXICAN BURROWING FROG

Rhinophrynus dorsalis
This frog may have a strange-looking shape, but it is
perfectly adapted to its home underground in a burrow.
It only comes to the surface to breed when there
are significant rainstorms and flooding. It even eats
underground where it dines on ants and termites.

20

HORNED FROG

Ceratophyrs sp.

The frogs on these two pages are named for the horns at the top of their eyes. The horns help them blend into the leaves on the forest floor where they live. Their huge mouths have given them another common name: Pacman Frogs. They use these large mouths to eat anything that can fit in including lizards, other frogs and even small rodents.

BUDGETT'S FROG

Lepidobatrachus laevis
This large-mouthed frog eats anything it can fit into its mouth but it uses its mouth in another way, too. When it feels threatened, it puffs itself up and opens its wide mouth and screams! And if the potential predator doesn't back off, the Budgett's Frog has two large tooth-like fangs on its bottom jaw to defend itself.

STRIPELESS TREE FROG

Hyla meridionalis
Stripeless Tree Frogs are usually a bright green color, but not this individual. Sometimes these frogs end up being bright blue, but no one really knows why. Whatever the reason for the color, it certainly makes this frog stand out.

NATTERJACK TOAD

Epidalea calamita
This toad often lives in sandy areas, including along the coast. It has very short legs, even for a toad, so instead of hopping, it moves forward in a fast crawl. Natterjack Toads may live in burrows but, unlike most other toad species, it digs them with its front feet, not its back feet.

AMAZON MILK FROG

Trachycephalus resinifictrix
The Amazon Milk Frog gets its name from a milky substance that it can exude from its skin when it feels threatened. The slime is poisonous and sticky and can cause pain if it gets into the predator's eyes. This is a young Amazon Milk Frog; they get less blue as they get older.

SOLOMON ISLANDS LEAF FROG

Ceratobatrachus guentheri
As its name suggests, this frog is shaped like a leaf and found in the Solomon Islands in Papua New Guinea. The projections on its eyes and nose help it take on an overall leaf shape and the ridges on its back look like leaf veins. These frogs are usually mottled brown, but some, like this one, can be yellow.

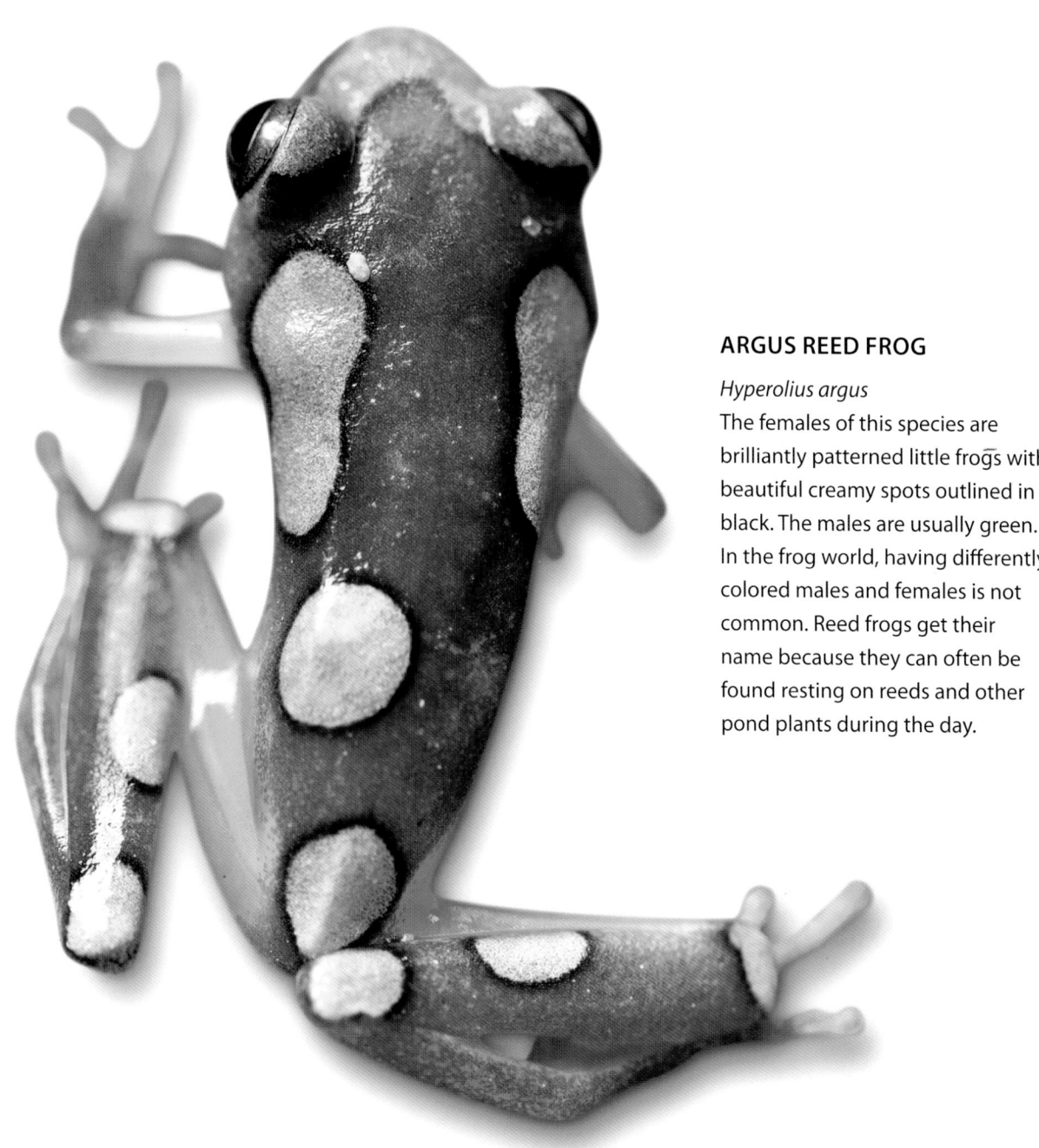

ARGUS REED FROG

Hyperolius argus

The females of this species are brilliantly patterned little frogs with beautiful creamy spots outlined in black. The males are usually green. In the frog world, having differently colored males and females is not common. Reed frogs get their name because they can often be found resting on reeds and other pond plants during the day.

RED-EYED LEAF FROG

Agalychnis callidryas
This is probably the world's most famous frog species because it has been used widely as a symbol of the rainforest. Red-eyed Leaf Frogs lay their eggs on twigs that overhang water. When the tadpoles hatch, they drop from the twig and fall into the pond below.

PYGMY MARSUPIAL FROG

Flectonotus pygmaeus

The female Pygmy Marsupial Frog carries her eggs on her back in pouches on her skin. She deposits the eggs in small cavities of water where they hatch and then develop into froglets. In some marsupial frog species (marsupial is a word usually used for mammals with a pouch such as kangaroos), the young develop in the egg and emerge from the egg on their mother's back as fully formed tiny frogs.

30

DARWIN'S FROG

Rhinoderma darwinii

This pointy-nosed frog is one of two species of Mouth-brooding Frog. Male Darwin's Frogs guard up to 40 eggs that are laid on land by the female. When the embryos in the eggs start to move, the male frog gobbles them up and keeps them safe in his vocal sac. The tadpoles develop into froglets inside the eggs and then hatch in the vocal sac. The froglets then crawl out of the eggs into their dad's mouth and jump out when he opens up.

GRAY TREE FROG

Hyla versicolor

Compared to other tree frogs, this one doesn't seem very weird, but it might be the weirdest frog of all. This tree frog is the master of color change for camouflage. They can be colored brilliant leaf green, mottled rock grey and rich bark brown. This tree frog also lives much farther north than most tree frog species and it can survive being frozen for months under the snow.

RAIN FROG

Breviceps sp.

These burrowing frogs have an interesting breeding strategy. They live in dry areas and stay buried underground until it rains. They then emerge from their burrows, find a mate and burrow underground together. The female lays her eggs in the burrow. The baby frogs develop in the eggs and then dig themselves out after they hatch.

BEAUTIFUL PYGMY FROG

Microhyla pulchra
If there was a prize for the animal looking
the most like a polished rock, the well-named
Beautiful Pygmy Frog would win. The pointed
nose of this frog gives it and its close relatives
another common name, the Narrow-mouthed Frogs.

CINNAMON FROG

Nyctixalus pictus

Instead of breeding in a pond, this frog's tadpoles develop in water that has collected in cavities in trees. These temporary water nurseries don't have predators such as fish that could eat the tadpoles. Because space in such sites is usually limited, there are usually only a few tadpoles in each hole.

GLASS FROG

Family Centrolenidae
It's obvious that the glass frogs on these two pages are very well named. From below, you can see into their bodies and study their veins, bones and internal organs. From above, this transparency helps them blend into whatever surface they are on. There are almost 150 different species of glass frog.

BLACK-SPOTTED CASQUE-HEADED TREE FROG

Trachycephalus nigromaculatus
Different frogs in the same pond may have different breeding strategies. The Black-spotted Casque-headed Tree Frog males call for mates only after a heavy rain. Other frogs sing on most nights during the rainy season but in one species the males call only after the first heavy rain at the beginning of the rainy season.

RED-LEGGED RUNNING FROG

Kassina maculata
As its name suggests, the Red-legged Running Frog runs instead of jumps. It also walks and has a gait in between a walk and a run that looks like a gallop. This fascinating frog is found from Kenya to South Africa in eastern Africa.

STICKY FROG

Kalophrynus sp.
This little frog gets its name from the sticky substances
it exudes when threatened. But it is the tadpole nursery
that makes this species really weird. The female frog
lays its eggs in carnivorous pitcher plants! Pitcher plants
hold liquid and secrete digestive enzymes to digest
insects that fall in. How the tadpoles stop the plant from
digesting them is a mystery.

HOLY CROSS TOAD

Notaden bennettii
Another burrowing toad, this species encases itself into a cocoon underground during dry periods, only emerging when it rains. These frogs have very short limbs, so the males produce a sticky substance that they use to attach themselves to a female during mating. In wet conditions this glue is so strong that scientists are studying it for use in reattaching broken tendons to bones!

MARBLED WOOD FROG

Batrachyla antartandica
This beautiful frog lays its eggs on the ground under
logs and in moss. The tadpoles live in flood waters
that rise over the egg laying site. Marbled Wood
Frogs are found in Chile and Argentina.

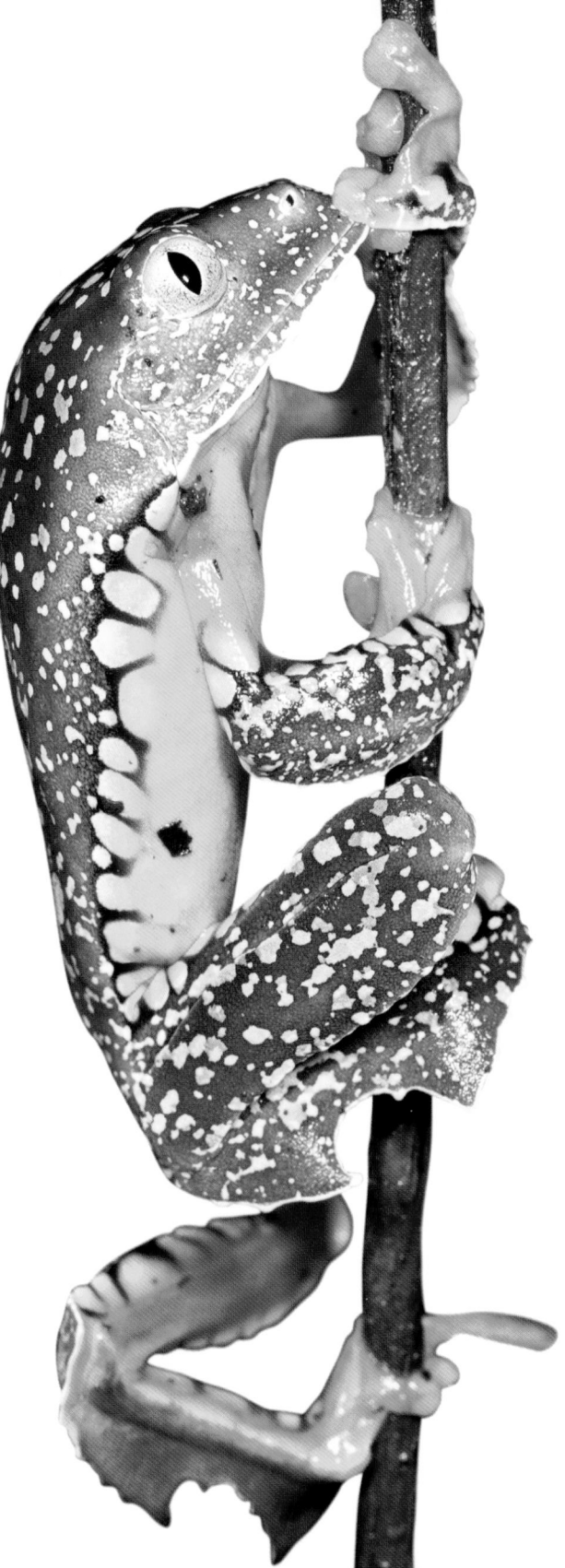

FRINGED LEAF FROG

Cruziohyla craspedopus
Another well-named species, the Fringed
Leaf Frog has conspicuous fringes on its hind
legs and its lips. It also has extra-large fingers
and big discs on its toes. This, along with the
brilliant orange belly and speckled blue back,
makes it one of the world's most spectacular
looking frogs.

RIO CHINGUAL VALLEY TREE FROG

Hyloscirtus pantostictus
This gorgeous frog is, unfortunately,
an endangered species. It is found in
the cloud forests of southern Colombia
and northern Ecuador where it is
threatened with the loss of its habitat
due to agricultural development,
logging and human settlement.

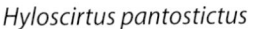

VIETNAMESE MOSSY FROG

Theloderma corticale
Instead of brightly advertising a toxic protection strategy like the poison dart frogs, to escape its enemies the Vietnamese Mossy Frog just stops moving — and disappears. Not only does it have a mottled green coloration, even its eyes blend in, it has projections and bumps all over its body that mimic the texture of moss.

TOMATO FROG

Dyscophus antongilii

It's not hard to see how this frog received its common name! The bright colors tell predators that this species does not make a good meal. But if a predator does try to take a bite, this frog produces a sticky substance that gums up the predator's mouth so the frog can get away.

AUSTRALIAN GREEN TREE FROG

Litoria caerulea

This fat frog can live near houses and sometimes even inside them. Once inside, they are drawn to wet places and so they can be found in sinks and toilets. Their large size and loose skin has given them another common name: Dumpy Frog.

WESTERN BANJO FROG

Limnodynastes dorsalis
Frogs are known for the loud calls that they make during the breeding season. Trills, croaks, peeps, gulps and even "ribbits" are some of the calls made by different species of frogs. Banjo Frogs are named for their call, which sounds like someone has made a single pluck on a banjo string.

SHREVE'S SARAYACU TREE FROG

Dendropsophus sarayacuensis
This colorful tree frog has a fairly wide distribution and is found in Bolivia, Ecuador, Brazil, Peru and Colombia. The genus *Dendropsophus* contains almost 100 different species.

ITALIAN TREE FROG

Hyla intermedia

Like many other male frogs, singing male Italian Tree Frogs are subject to an interesting form of parasitism. As the male sings in a pond, other often smaller males may quietly wait nearby. When a female frog is attracted and moving towards the sound of the singing male, one of these smaller males may intercept her and mate with her, leaving the singing male to have done all the work but not get a mate.

WALLACE'S FLYING FROG

Rhacophorus nigropalmatus
Flying Frogs don't really fly, they glide. This and a few other species of frogs
are able to launch themselves from a high branch and coast down at least 70 m
without injury. This is a great way for them to escape from predators quickly.

LEMUR LEAF FROG

Hylomantis lemur

This frog has very prominent, vertical pupils. It is thought that vertical slit pupils are better at seeing horizontal movement and horizontal slit pupils are better at seeing vertical movement. This may mean that the different pupils are adaptations to seeing certain prey species, but no one has proven this theory yet.

BRIGHT-EYED FROG

Boophis doulioti
This frog of Madagascar shows how well frogs can blend in when they are asleep. By tucking its feet under its body and angling its head downwards, it looks like a bump on a tree branch. Some frog species even have a clear eyelid with a pattern on it to make the eye less distinctive when the frog is resting.

BRIGHT-EYED FROG

Boophis picturatus
There are approximately 70 species of *Boophis* frogs and they are
all found in Madagascar and the neighboring Comoros Islands.
They are often called Bright-eyed Frogs because of their brilliantly
colored eye patterns. Many of the members of this group are
semi-transparent, much like the South American Glass Frogs.

FOREST BRIGHT-EYED FROG

Boophis erythrodactylus
Most *Boophis* frogs are arboreal, meaning that they spend much of their time in the trees above ground. Some *Boophis* species, however, are found on the ground in savannah habitats. These ground species have smaller toe pads because they don't do as much climbing as the arboreal species.

COMMON SPADEFOOT TOAD

Pelobates fuscus
This toad gets its interesting name from a projection on its heel that it uses like a spade to dig. It scoops with one hind foot and then the other and slowly digs itself straight down. This toad spends much of its time underground except when it emerges to breed during heavy rains.

TAPICHALACA TREE FROG

Hyla tapichalaca
This alert looking frog with the white toes was
first discovered in 2003. When it was found, the frog
exuded a sticky, smelly, white fluid which likely helps
protect it from predators. It also displayed white patches
on its elbows, heels and stomach that may be a warning to predators as well.

PINE BARRENS TREE FROG

Hyla andersonii
This tree frog is limited to the pine barren areas of the eastern
United States. These areas tend to have acidic ponds and bogs
and so the Pine Barrens Tree Frog tadpoles are adapted to
surviving these low-pH conditions.

COCHRAN'S RUNNING FROG

Kassina cochranae

This running frog exudes defensive chemicals in its skin giving it an unpleasant odor and taste. While this likely protects the frog from many predators, there are still records of herons and snakes eating this species.

MADAGASCAN REED FROG

Heterixalus madagascariensis
It only takes approximately six months from
the time this species hatches from its egg until
it is large enough to breed. This works well
in its Madagascan home where it appears to
breed throughout the year. Madagascan Reed
Frogs can be blue, yellow or white.

TRICOLOR REED FROG

Heterixalus tricolor
Another reed frog from Madagascar, the Tricolor
Reed Frog is sometimes found on a plant called
a Screw Pine. This plant can hold water at
the base of its leaves and some Madagascar
frogs are dependant on Screw Pines for
their breeding cycle but Tricolor Reed
Frogs may just use the water to
stay moist.

YUCATAN CASQUE-HEADED TREE FROG

Triprion petasatus
This tree frog is also called the Shovel-nosed
Frog for obvious reasons. But what isn't obvious
is why its head is shaped that way.

CENTRAL BRIGHT-EYED FROG

Boophis rappiodes

This arboreal *Boophis* frog has well-developed toe pads to help it climb. It hunts mostly at night so during the day it hides amongst the vegetation like other tree frogs. It lives beside forest streams where it lays its eggs during the breeding season.

INDEX